For my most wonderful
friend, Cathy.

May all your days
be filled with good
friends, laughter,
wine and CATS!

love,
Sherry

The
Cat Lovers'
Book
of Days

The Cat Lovers' Book of Days

WITH ILLUSTRATIONS FROM
THE METROPOLITAN MUSEUM OF ART
NEW YORK

Hugh Lauter Levin Associates, Inc.

DISTRIBUTED BY
MACMILLAN PUBLISHING COMPANY
NEW YORK

INTRODUCTION

Cats—intriguing, independent, individualistic—have been enriching our lives for centuries. Their effect on human beings is unparalleled. We find felines fascinating, finicky, and fun. What other animal can be so aloof one minute and so loving the next?

The Cat Lovers' Book of Days is a permanent record that can be used year after year because dates are not assigned to days of the week. The book is beautifully illustrated with works of art that feature cats from The Metropolitan Museum of Art in New York City. The compendium of a variety of cat facts, lore, and musings is followed by calendar, address and Visits to the Vet pages. With your personal entries, this will be a very special book that you will enjoy and treasure.

JANUARY

A nose-to-nose greeting between cats means,
"Do I know you?" even when they do. Cats do
the same thing with people they like.

1

One difference between cats and dogs is that
dogs sit when told; cats only if it is convenient.

2

Some Chinese believe that the time of day can
be determined by lifting up a cat's eyelid and
noting the size of the pupil.

3

A falling cat does not always land on its feet, as
many people believe.

4

Cats have large eyes in relation to the size of
their bodies. The smaller the cat, the more
prominent its eyes.

5

SPRING PLAY IN A T'ANG GARDEN *(detail). Style of Hsüan-tsung (Chinese,
1398–1435); 18th century. Handscroll, colors on silk; 14¾ × 104 in.
Fletcher Fund, 1947, 47.18.9*

January

6 Ancient Greeks believed that the cat was created by the moon.

7 Learn to manipulate your cat or it will manipulate you.

8 Cats can be protected from most severe diseases, such as feline distemper, by immunizing vaccinations.

9 Cats' loose skin makes it easy for them to wriggle out of trouble.

10 "The rat stops still when the eyes of the cat shine."
—*Madagascan saying*

11 Siamese kittens are white at birth.

12 In 59 B.C., a Roman official sent to Egypt inadvertently killed a cat and was hanged.

By and large, the best plaything for a cat is another cat.

13

Approximately 1,000 cats compete for ribbons and trophies at the International Cat Show held annually at Madison Square Garden.

14

With about 15 more vertebrae than a human's, a cat's backbone can flex, extend, or twist up to 180 degrees.

15

A catnap, a short light snooze, was created by the cat.

16

French folklore has it that if a black cat is tied to where five roads meet, it will run to hidden treasure when released.

17

When suckling, a cat learns to knead. It is a habit it carries into adulthood and signifies contentment.

18

"Happy owner, happy cat. Indifferent owner, reclusive cat."
—*Chinese proverb*

19

·SAID THE CAT-·

20

"When I play with my cat, who knows whether she diverts herself with me or I with her."
—*Michel de Montaigne*

21

One who loves cats is called an ailurophile.

22

Cats were highly prized in countries where rodents were a plague and cats a rarity. Anyone convicted of killing a cat had to give its owner a sheep and lamb.

23

A hiding place or retreat is essential to most cats when complete privacy is needed.

24

Maine coon cats are large, chunky, long-haired cats that were a favorite of the late actress, Bette Davis.

25

Some cats act perversely for seemingly no reason. They disgrace you in front of your friends or attach themselves to the one person in the room who detests them.

26

Cats don't like cold food; they prefer meals at room temperature.

SAID THE CAT, Charles Henry Bennett *(English, 1829–1867); from* The Sorrowful Ending of Noodledoo, with the Fortunes and Fate of Her Neighbours and Friends*, London, 1865. Hand-colored commercial printing; 8 × 6½ in. Rogers Fund, 1906; Thomas J. Watson Library*

January

27
L'Enfant et les Sortilèges, Maurice Ravel's children's opera, contains a duet for male and female cat.

28
The fictional Puss in Boots was so clever that he killed an ogre and won his master a fortune and a princess.

29
"Dogs remember faces, cats places."
  —*English saying*

30
The glossy sheen of a short-haired cat's coat is enhanced by gently rubbing it with a piece of silk, velvet, or chamois cloth.

31
The Havana Brown cat—the color of an expensive Cuban cigar—has a solid, dark brown, short-haired coat. Its body is slim, fine-boned, and elegantly muscular.

FEBRUARY

The American songbird known as a catbird is noted for its mewing call.

1

"If you are worthy of its affection, a cat will be your friend, but never your slave."
  —*Théophile Gautier*

2

Smells that cats find irresistible include asparagus, mint, eucalyptus, and mimosa.

3

Purebred cats are classified into three types: natural, man-made, and spontaneous mutation. Persians are natural; Ocicats are man-made hybrids; the Manx is a mutation.

4

Guy de Maupassant, J. K. Huysmans, and Anatole France, it is reported, needed the presence of a cat in order to work.

5

Although cats are not as athletically inclined as dogs, when required they can be speedy and agile.

6

Teach a cat to come in from outdoors or another room by calling its name before it is fed.

7

8

Cats are honored in dance in Peter Ilyich Tchaikowsky's *The Sleeping Beauty* with a pas-de-deux for Puss in Boots and the White Cat.

9

Whiskers on the chin are unnecessary for cats because they don't root around for food or prey.

10

The cat first appeared in China around 1000 B.C. It was thought to bring good luck and happiness to the family.

11

"Honest as the cat when the meat is out of reach."
   —*English saying*

12

Blind and deaf for the first week of life, a kitten's sense of smell keeps it close to its mother and her milk.

13

Soft, spongy pads and tufts of hair on its paws muffle sounds when a cat stalks its prey and are shock absorbers when it is leaping.

14

The Siamese cat, although small and delicate in stature, is known to be a ferocious fighter.

GIRL MAKING A GARLAND, Hans Süss von Kulmbach *(German, c. 1480–1521/22); c. 1508. Tempera and oil on wood; 7 × 5½ in. Gift of J. Pierpont Morgan, 1917, 17.190.21*

February

15

A feline's whiskers, eyebrows, toes, paws, and hairs on the inner ear surface all serve as organs of touch.

16

The Greek word "kattos"—cat—appears in Aristophanes's *Acharnians*, around 425 B.C.

17

"The cat laps the moonbeams in the bowl of water, thinking them to be milk."
—*Hindu saying*

18

Often the easiest way to give a cat medication is to mix it with food.

19

Kittens and puppies brought up in the same home usually become fast friends, playing and even sleeping together.

20

A cat spends two-thirds of its life snoozing, the other third in hunting, grooming, playing and, if it has the chance, loving.

21

A 9-year old tomcat named Spice weighed in at 43 pounds on June 26, 1974, in Ridgefield, Connecticut. The average weight of an adult cat is 11 pounds.

It is better to pick up a cat, rather than call it, if you are going to reprimand it or put it into a traveling case.

22

Recent studies suggest that cats can differentiate colors; however, it is not clear if they can distinguish between red and yellow.

23

A female tabby in Devon, England, called Ma, lived to be 34 years old.

24

Colette's cats, such as Fanchette, Zwerga, and La Chatte, are immortalized in the famous French writer's works.

25

One who hates or fears cats is called an ailurophobe.

26

Cat burglars are lithe, agile felons who are adept at entering and leaving the burglary scene without attracting attention.

27

A Persian cat needs daily brushing and combing. Once a week a specially prepared cat grooming powder, or a talcum powder and cornstarch mixture, will give the coat body.

28/29

MARCH

Mythology has attributed the cat with the power to control the sun's rays.

1

Most felines adore sweet scents and abhor bad smells. Don't be surprised to see them lolling in your favorite flower bed or tiptoeing among your toiletries.

2

Kittens are fascinated by walking on a piano keyboard and seem to take special delight in the resonant vibrations of the bass keys.

3

Jean Cocteau learned to admire cats through his association with Colette.

4

"A cat is a lion in a jungle of small bushes."
—*English proverb*

5

MY LITTLE WHITE KITTIES INTO MISCHIEF *(detail)*. Currier & Ives, publishers *(American, 1857–1907). Hand-colored lithograph; 8¼ × 12½ in. with border. Bequest of Adele S. Colgate, 1962, 63.550.479*

March

6

With the ability to relax completely, the cat's every action is calculated to promote its own well-being.

7

Cats love to bask in patches of sunlight.

8

It is reported that Samuel Johnson personally shopped for oysters for his beloved cat Hodge.

9

The three Brontë sisters loved cats, and the diaries of Charlotte and Anne often refer to their favorite felines.

10

Unlike the dog, the imprint of man upon the cat has had little influence on its behavior.

11

Your cat's name may tell more about you than it does about your cat.

12

The Korat, Russian Blue, and Chartreux cats are genetically related by color of coat and skin. The color may vary from light to dark gray, with dark shading.

13

Three would-be world conquerors—Hitler, Napoleon, and Alexander the Great—were ailurophobes.

14

Edgar Allan Poe utilized the mysteries of the cat in his tale *The Black Cat*, in which a cat exposes a murderer.

15

Cats evolved by natural selection to hunt rodents. Programmed by nature, they will respond to the sound of crinkling paper as if it were mice rustling in their burrows.

16

The tail of a cat has a language all its own and can communicate contentment or preparation for attack.

17

When a cat feels doubt or fear, it finds comfort through grooming itself.

18

"The cat in gloves catches no mice."
—*Benjamin Franklin*

19

A cat's litter can have more than one father, which is why the kittens may come in various color combinations.

It was not until the 18th century that cats became primary subjects in paintings.

20

Because of the cat's identification with the sun, in some cultures the string-on-fingers game called "cat's cradle" is thought to control the sun's movements.

21

Catarina was a large tortoiseshell who shared Edgar Allan Poe's impoverished life.

22

Cat "training" is well nigh impossible, but food bribes may work if they're offered as rewards for a desired behavior.

23

Domestic cats are divided into long-haired and short-haired varieties.

24

The distinctive voice of a Siamese cat sounds much like the howl of a baby; it uses its voice in lengthy conversations with people.

25

A cat fed a meatless diet soon will become ill and die a painful death.

26

MOTHER, CHILD, AND CAT, *Unknown designer of the Wiener Werkstätte, Austrian, founded 1905. Color lithograph postcard; 5½ × 3½ in. Museum Accession*

March

27

"The dog for the man, the cat for the woman."
—*English proverb*

28

The cat possesses hundreds of muscles that enable its body to perform with a minimum of effort and a maximum of efficiency.

29

The elegant, extended stretch of a cat may be a form of low-energy isometric exercise.

30

The Tonkinese ranks high on the people-loving cat scale. It is a hybrid result from crossing a Siamese to a Burmese.

31

Empty cartons or pie tins can be stacked in places where you don't want a cat. The movement and clatter caused when a cat touches them will scare it off.

On the average, each cat has about 12 whiskers, arranged in four rows, on each side of its nose.

1

"The ideal of calm exists in a sitting cat."
—*Jules Reynard*

2

Mother cats teach kittens to hunt by bringing a live mouse home and letting them "play" with the prey.

3

Plutarch explains that the dilation and contraction of cats' pupils at night corresponds to the waxing and waning of the moon.

4

While the forward, arched position of cats' claws enable them to scale a tree with grace, they make the descent awkward, so the cat must slither down, rear end first.

5

"A lame cat is better than a swift horse when rats infest the palace."
—*Proverb*

6

In ancient Egypt when a household cat died, family members would shave their eyebrows in mourning. The dead cat was placed in a sheet, embalmed, and deposited in a sacred vault.

7

Often cats pause to admire themselves in mirrors. Sometimes they even look behind the mirror to find the "other cat."

8

A cat in Bonham, Texas, reputedly delivered her 420th kitten when she was 17 years old.

9

Cats have been known to attack poisonous snakes. They're faster than their prey and can worry a snake until all the danger is wrung out of it.

10

The Japanese imported cats from China in the 10th century and limited their ownership to the nobility.

11

It's been reported that cats furiously washing are "predicting" rain.

12

THE WATCHFUL CAT *(detail)*. John Alonzo Williams *(American, 1869–1947). Watercolor on cardboard; 12¼ × 17⅜ in. Gift of A. J. Hammerslough, 1940, 40.17*

April

13

Domenico Scarlatti's piano piece, *The Cat's Fugue*, is said to represent a cat padding across a keyboard.

14

A cat has 30 adult teeth and a rough tongue that helps it clean particles from its fur.

15

A cat purrs when it's happy, meows when it wants attention, and is silent when planning its next move.

16

Most cats don't like getting wet but are fascinated by water movement and will sit for long periods watching a tap drip.

17

Independence is the most admired quality of the cat in modern times.

18

"Rumpies," "stumpies," and "longies"—references to the status of the tail—are nicknames for Cymric and Manx cats.

19

Two cats, Hellcat and Brownie, were the sole heirs to the $415,000 estate of Dr. William Grier of San Diego, California, when he died in 1963.

20

Albert Schweitzer sought relaxation in two ways: his music and his cats.

21

Blue Persians have tabby markings at birth.

22

Felines' fastidious behavior makes them easy to housebreak when their litter pan is routinely cleaned.

23

Cats live longer than most other small pets. The average life span is about 15 years, although some cats have lived well into their twenties.

24

You will be rich or lucky in love if you find one white hair on a black cat, according to a legend in Brittany.

25

Cats will always lie soft."
—*Theocritus*

26

In early Christian times, superstitions about cats were rampant; they could sour milk, foretell the future, and bring rain and good harvests.

ome people with rheumatism think that cat
ur can cure them and encourage a cat to
tretch out on them.

27

iver, which should be cooked, is enjoyed by
many cats and can be used as a special treat
once a week.

28

"The familiars of Witches do most ordinarily
appear in the shape of cats ... this beast is
dangerous in soul and body."
—*Edward Topsell*

29

he Scottish Fold is a recent mutation that was
born in a litter of normal-eared kittens at a
arm near Dundee, Scotland, in the 1960s. The
at's ears fold forward and downward.

30

HAREM SCENE AT COURT OF SHAH JAHAN *(detail). Unknown artist (Indian,
second quarter 17th century); Mughal period. Album leaf, ink, colors,
and gold on paper; entire sheet 13⅛ × 8¼ in. Theodore M. Davis
Collection, Bequest of Theodore M. Davis, 1915, 30.95.174, no. 26*

MAY

1

A cat's ears turn 10 times quicker in the direction of sound than those of the best watchdog.

2

Mohammed was so fond of his cat that it is said he cut off the sleeve on which his cat was sleeping rather than disturb it.

3

It is a display of great trust for a cat to roll over and, completely relaxed, expose its stomach.

4

Pedigreed cats are judged on a 100-point scale that has been developed for standards of the cat's color class and breed status.

5

Body language is used by cats when they are "talking" to one another. Sounds are saved for communicating with people.

children in England used to be encouraged to play with a tortoiseshell cat because it was thought to help develop powers of clairvoyance.

6

Cats have a good sense of time. Some know their owners' routines so well, they wake them before the alarm clock rings.

7

"It is with the approach of winter that cats ... wear their richest fur and assume an air of sumptuous and delightful opulence."
—*Pierre Loti*

8

It's easy to get a cat's attention by feigning a falsetto voice.

9

A belief of Japanese sailors is that three-colored cats (white, red, and black) can foretell storms.

10

If not allowed outdoors, cats' natural hunting instincts will be acted out with toy mice, erasers, socks, or other small objects.

11

A playful, alert, and curious kitten, who will follow you about when you set it on the floor, has the potential for growing into a satisfying companion pet.

12

13

tudies show that living with a cat can reduce
lood pressure and calm an overworked heart.

14

ogs have to be taught to bring their masters a
tick or a ball, but cats will bring you
omething voluntarily and lay it at your feet as
 present.

15

uperstition has it that warts can be removed
y rubbing them with a male tortoiseshell's tail
. but only in May.

16

ven when in deep sleep, a cat can be
wakened easily by touch or sound.

17

oologists have described the cat as a
asterpiece of construction, perfect in its
ombination of efficiency and grace.

18

f man could be crossed with the cat, it would
mprove man but deteriorate the cat."
 —*Mark Twain*

19

 haw, or third eyelid, moves diagonally across
 cat's eye; its presence can signify illness.

ARPER'S MAY, Edward Penfield *(American, 1866–1925); 1896.
olor lithograph poster; 20 × 14 in. Museum Accession, 1957,
7.627.9 (37)*

May

20
The ballet *Les Demoiselles de la Nuit* tells of a white cat's transformation into a woman and her final return to the cat world.

21
A cat has five senses of taste: bitter, sour, sweet, salt, and water.

22
If a cat rejects medication that has been mixed with its food, wrap the cat snugly in a towel, immobilizing it, and quickly poke the pill down its throat.

23
"As long as a cat will play, it's okay."
    —*Southern saying*

24
At cat shows, categories often include Longest Whiskers, Splashiest Color and Owner/Pet Look-alike.

25
If given the chance, a healthy cat will hunt 6 to 8 hours out of its 24-hour day.

26
When a cat is moved to a new locale, don't let it outside for a few weeks; it could wander or try to find its way back to its former home.

he birth weight of a kitten is usually three to
ve ounces.

ed cats, sometimes called ginger or
marmalade, are almost always male.

The cat lives alone, has no need of society,
beys only when she pleases . . . pretends to
leep that she may see the more clearly . . . ."
   —*Chateaubriand*

When you first get a cat, give it a box or place
o call its own. It will like it or move to where
t is more comfortable.

Among purebred cats, the Himalayan is a
veritable "glamor puss." It combines the dense,
ong fur of the Persian with the varied coat
olors and startling blue eyes of the Siamese.

JUNE

A sty in the eye, some English believe, can be cured by rubbing it with a tomcat's tail.

1

Nine, representing the trinity of trinities, was considered a lucky number in ancient times. The cat, too, was lucky and thought to have nine lives.

2

The writer William Rose Bénet tells the story of an amazing cat who conducts music with his tail in *The King of Cats*.

3

Cats respond better to women's voices because women's voices are usually higher pitched than men's.

4

Black Persians are born brown.

5

June

6

The term "cat's-paw," meaning a dupe, is derived from a fable where a monkey used a sleeping cat's paw to retrieve hot chestnuts from the fire.

7

If a family in the Ozarks keeps black cats around the house, all daughters in the house will be old maids.

8

"A cat's a cat and that's that."
—*American folk saying*

9

A favorite pose is the "hunker," with all four feet tucked under or the "sit-up," with tail furled around its bottom.

10

Cats walk on their toes with their claws retracted, leaving no clear footprints for any pursuers to follow.

11

"The cat is in the clock," is an old Flemish phrase that refers to a quarrelsome family.

12

The criteria for judging a Blue Persian will include: size and shape of head and eyes; color; type; eye color; coat; balance and refinement.

Dry cat food helps keep a cat's teeth healthy and its breath fresh.

13

A cat can be trained to walk on a leash if you accustom it to a harness at about four months.

14

An indoor cat rubbing its chin along a coffee table is marking its territory as surely as one marking a fencepost in your backyard.

15

During his lifetime, a good Hindu must feed at least one cat.

16

Cat lovers are rewarded by the feline sensitivity that causes a cat to snuggle in your lap when you are sick or lonely.

17

By nature cats don't find sweet foods very attractive; in fact, they tend to avoid them.

18

For its relatively small size, felines are both agile and powerful; brain, nerves, and muscles are coordinated in machinelike precision.

19

20

"It has been the providence of nature to give this creature nine lives instead of one."
—*Proverb*

21

Cats are the cleanest of all domestic animals. Their washing and grooming rituals are carried out with compulsive energy.

22

In Morrisburg, Louisiana, cats are prohibited from chasing ducks down a city street.

23

Some cats fear men and run from them. It is usually because of a bad experience, possibly with a male veterinarian, in the past.

24

There is a new breed of cat, still unnamed, that has exceptionally short legs.

25

Grass, which is indigestible, is eaten by a cat when it wants to get rid of a hairball or anything else in its stomach.

26

There are almost 60 million cats in the United States, outnumbering dogs by 10 million.

SPRING PLAY IN A T'ANG GARDEN *(detail). Style of Hsüan-tsung (Chinese, 1398–1435); 18th century. Handscroll, colors on silk; 14¾ × 104 in. Fletcher Fund, 1947, 47.18.9*

June

27

Japanese lore includes some demon cats, but most often tales are about cats who perform kind deeds; artists drew them with love and sensitivity.

28

"Cats are a mysterious kind of folk. There is more passing in their minds than we are aware of."
—*Sir Walter Scott*

29

John Gay casts the cat as an astute mouser in his satiric fables of the 18th century royal court of England.

30

The Ocicat is a recently developed hybrid breed resulting from crossing the Siamese and Abyssinian cat. With its spotted coat and sleek body, it resembles a small ocelot.

urrhaps, an Abyssinian, won Best of Show in
987 at the International Cat Show—after
issing all the judges.

1

ats regained favor in the middle of the 17th
entury. Cardinal Richelieu kept dozens of
hem at court and left endowments for those
urviving him.

2

calico is a tortoiseshell with white who looks,
ccording to one saying, as if she's fallen into a
ucket of milk.

3

Many zoologists agree that a cat's first year is
qual to 15 human years. When a cat is 7, its
ge is 50; when it's 10, it's 60; at 15 it's 75.

4

elines run only when necessary or when they
vant to let off steam.

5

July

Tiny spines, which give a cat's tongue a rough, scratchy texture, help it scoop up liquids when it drinks.

6

Dogs are ready to romp when their masters tell them to; cats only when they feel like it.

7

Some people in the Philippines say that cats eat coconut meat because long ago the coconut used to be the head of a cat.

8

There once was a law that a cat on the street after dark in Berea, Ohio, had to display a red tail light.

9

In Belgium during the Inquisition, cats were thrown from the tops of towers to purge evil spirits.

10

An old British saying declares, "Whenever the cat of the house is black, the lasses of lovers will have no lack."

11

Creatures of habit, cats are easily upset by changes in routine and don't mind showing it.

12

THE LITTLE PETS . Currier & Ives, *publishers (American, 1857–1907). Hand-colored lithograph; 12 × 9 in. Bequest of Adele S. Colgate, 1962, 63.550.333*

July

13
At one time, it was illegal to own both a cat and a bird in Reed City, Michigan.

14
Cats' long face whiskers resemble the tactile barbels that hang from certain fishes' lips, explaining their common name—catfish.

15
Japanese ships have more cats on board than any other country's ships.

16
Cats were first domesticated by man at least 8,000 years ago.

17
The feline's ear has approximately 30 muscles, while the human ear, which barely moves at all, scarcely has a half-dozen.

18
The tabby or striped cat usually has an "M" on its forehead.

19
Cats can walk along fences and narrow ledges because their front legs swing inward so that their feet are positioned in a line, one in front of the other.

20

ome cats lead multiple lives, claiming several
omes as theirs, with the involved families not
aving a clue.

21

The cat is a dilettante in fur."
—*Théophile Gautier*

22

was said in the Middle Ages that witches
onned cast-off cat skins to ride their brooms
o midnight orgies.

23

on't give cats any bones. Cooking makes
ones too brittle and ingestion can cause
itestinal damage.

24

a the Victorian era, especially among the
fluent, a cat figure became a "must" in
rawing-room decor.

25

he Cornish Rex, with an oily wavy coat, is an
xcellent cat for people with allergies.

26

Then a feline rubs up against you, it is
narking you with its scent. Cats that are
riendly mark each other in the same way.

27

Isaac Newton, mindful that his cats hated doors, invented the cat flap so they could come and go at will.

28

In Lemonine, Montana, cats must wear three bells as a warning to birds.

29

Cats do not appear in the earliest cave and rock art because they were not a source of game or danger to prehistoric people.

30

A cat reveals its traits through its eyes. They reflect gentleness, wisdom, violence, serenity, and cunning.

31

Persians, previously called Angoras, have a long silky coat, stocky bodies, short legs, a broad rounded head, a ruff around the neck, round eyes, and a short full tail.

CAT IN WINDOW, Utagawa Hiroshige *(Japanese, 1797–1858); from* One Hundred Famous Views of Edo. *Wood-block print, colors on paper; 13⅛ × 8¾ in. (margins trimmed). Rogers Fund, 1914, 60*

AUGUST

1

The best tranquilizer for someone in an agitated state is stroking a cat. It's not easy to stay tense with a cat in your lap, and it can lower your blood pressure, too.

2

The hairless Sphynx has been likened to a soft suede hot-water bottle.

3

Cats have their own air conditioning. When they lick their fur, they deposit a fine layer of saliva that evaporates and keeps them cool on warm days.

4

Cats have been living with people and sharing their lives for 5,000 years, half as long as dogs.

5

A cat collar should always have an elastic insert so that a cat can wriggle out of it if the collar gets caught on something.

Cats barely tolerate wearing bells and ribbons.

6

An errant dog grovels and begs forgiveness; a chastised cat stalks off and washes itself.

7

Cats' imprint on sea lore is seen in such expressions as "catwalk," meaning a narrow passageway; "cathead," where the anchor is hoisted; and "cat-o'-nine-tails," a whip.

8

Except for its medium-long, double coat, the Cymric is identical to the Manx.

9

Catnip grows wild or can be cultivated in pots. Dry leaves and pet toys stuffed with the plant are sold in pet stores.

10

When a cat's ears are pointed forward, it is expressing happiness and expectancy; when its ears are flat against its head, it is angry.

11

The first major cat show was organized by the English illustrator and cat lover, Harrison Weir. It was held at the Crystal Palace in London in 1871.

12

13

Charles Dickens had a warm attachment to a kitten who craved affection. It would curl up in his lap while he wrote or read.

14

Before it goes outside at night, a cat will pause in the doorway in order to let its eyes become accustomed to the darkness.

15

When traveling, don't feed your cat eight hours before leaving and don't give it water two hours before departure time.

16

When embarrassed, a cat that is walking may stop and groom itself. Scientists call this "displacement activity."

17

The cat-headed goddess, Bast, was worshipped by a prehistoric clan in Bubastis, Egypt, as far back as 4000 to 10,000 B.C.

18

In Natchez, Mississippi, a law prohibits cats from drinking beer.

19

A cat falls asleep very easily.

MANCHU CAT *(detail). Unknown artist (Chinese, c. 1821–1850); Ch'ing Dynasty. Theater curtain, wool flannel, silk, metal; 10 ft. 8¾ in. × 6 ft. 8 in. Gift of Fong Chow, 1959, 59.190*

August

20

One reason a cat likes to lie on your chest is that it picks up the comforting sound of your heartbeat.

21

A favorite feline position is curling up in a circle, sometimes with one paw over its eyes, as if to shut out the light.

22

In Don Marquis' *archie and mehitabel*, mehitabel, the cat who says she was Cleopatra in a former life, "would sell her soul for a plate of fish."

23

Feline sleep falls into three categories: the brief nap, the longer light sleep, and the deep sleep.

24

The Siamese is judged on: coat texture and color of points and body; type and shape of body; color, shape and type of eyes; type and shape of head; ears; legs and paws; condition; and tail.

25

One place the agile cat cannot reach is the top of its head between the ears, so a human stroke there is appreciated.

26

"No matter how much cats fight, there always seem to be plenty of kittens."
—*Abraham Lincoln*

Ernest Hemingway's home in Key West, Florida, where he lived with 50 cats, is now a museum where descendants of the writer's cats are visited by the public.

27

Threatened by a dog, a cat will display its largest size by arching its back, stiffening its legs, bristling its fur, and standing broadside toward the "enemy."

28

A tortoiseshell is black and orange; a "true tortoiseshell" has each color in larger, distinguishable piebald patches.

29

For the stay-at-home cat there is a video of birds singing.

30

"One of the most startling differences between a cat and a lie is that a cat has only nine lives."
—*Mark Twain*

31

SEPTEMBER

While most cats accept a diet of prepared catfood, they—like humans—have been known to fancy less mundane delicacies, such as olives, tomatoes, or avocados.

1

Tortoiseshell and calico cats are nearly always female.

2

A group of young cats is called a kindle; groups of older cats are known as clusters or clowders.

3

Cats' eyes need only about one-sixth the amount of light we do.

4

Felines cannot bear to be laughed at.

5

L'HIVER: CHAT SUR UN COUSSIN ("Winter: Cat on a Cushion"); Théophile-Alexandre Steinlen *(French, 1859–1923). Color lithograph; 20 × 24 in. Gift of Henry J. Plantin, 1950, 50.616.9*

September

6

The best thing to do when a cat is up a tree is leave the scene and wait until it comes down of its own free will.

7

In March, 1991, Barbara, a cat in Hong Kong, survived a 50-story fall with only minor injuries when she fell from a penthouse onto a tin roof.

8

"Old cats mean young mice."
—*Italian saying*

9

The cat is a symbol of the good, plush, or luxurious life—hence, the phrase "fat cat."

10

Felines sleep around 18 hours a day and will entertain themselves by eating, playing, and staring out windows while you are away.

11

Cats don't like change and prize their familiar surroundings. If you go away, it's better to have somebody come to your home than to board the cat.

12

Often referred to as "Rajahs," Burmese cats are believed to have lived in Buddhist monasteries in Burma in the fifteenth century. They have long, slim legs and a coat that is short-haired.

September

In the 15th to 18th centuries, the Annunciation was the scene in which painters most often included a cat—though it was usually disinterested.

13

Studies show that cats use five vowels, nine consonants, two diphthongs, and one triphthong.

14

When choosing a new kitten to bring home, check for: clear, luminous eyes; a clean, glossy coat; clean ears with no odor; white teeth evenly set in pink gums; and a bouncy walk.

15

With about 67 million olfactory cells, a cat can detect smells we don't even know exist.

16

Dogs are social animals whose ancestors, wolves and jackals, lived in packs. Except for lions, wild cats are lone hunters.

17

The Abyssinian has the grace and appearance of a miniature mountain lion. It dotes on attention but will bolt for any door that opens to the outdoors. It is extremely energetic.

18

Winston Churchill was so attached to his tomcat that he personally took him to a safe place during the London blitz.

19

September

20

In China from 2205 to 225 B.C., sacrificial rites and ceremonies were held honoring cats, and heavy fines were imposed for destroying them.

21

Cats were doted upon by Queen Victoria and during her reign they came into great favor and were romanticized.

22

Once you've picked up a Ragdoll, you'll see how this limp, floppy feline got its name. A California native of the 1960s, it is a hybrid result of crossing a Birman with a Persian.

23

Cats newly arrived in the same household need time and space to become accustomed to each other.

24

If your cat can't go outside and won't use a scratching post, trim the tips of its front claws with nail clippers.

25

"The cat is the only animal which accepts the comforts but rejects the bondage of domesticity."
—*Georges de Buffon*

26

The "civet cat" is not a cat at all, but a small spotted skunk.

PUSSY'S RETURN *(detail).* Currier & Ives, *publishers (American, 1857–1907). Hand-colored lithograph; 8½ × 12½ in. Bequest of Adele S. Colgate, 1962, 63.550.314*

September

27
The elegant coat of a Siamese cat comes from a genetic trait; its pale color and darker points are a form of imperfect albinism.

28
Studies show that kittens begin to dream when they are around 10 days old.

29
"To please himself only, the cat purrs."
   —*Irish proverb*

30
Cats' long, pointed canine teeth are designed for stabbing prey. The molars are used like scissors blades to cut food into pieces small enough to swallow.

More than any other animal, cats are used in publicity and advertising in the media.

1

Fossil remains similar to those of the typical house cat first appeared in the Pliocene era, about 10,000,000 years ago.

2

When a cat is seriously fighting, it lies on its back, pulls its legs close to its body, and brings its claws into play, thus protecting the spine, its most vulnerable part.

3

A cat accommodates its sleeping positions; when it's cold, it is usually in a circle; when it's warm, its body is elongated.

4

It's documented that a cat left behind in New York found its way to its owner's new home in California after five months.

5

The Cheshire Cat in Lewis Carroll's *Alice in Wonderland* was famous for vanishing slowly, beginning with the end of its tail and ending with its grin.

6

"Psi trailing," or cats' ability to find their way home under extreme conditions, is a mystery to scientists.

7

Nothing is known of the ancestry of the Siamese-Burmese type of cat; possibly they are decendants of interbred oriental wild cats.

8

After a while cats in the same home form a bond and often groom each other and sleep together.

9

Philatelic cats have appeared in postage stamps issued at various times by Poland, Yemen, Cuba, Luxembourg, Rumania, Spain, Yugoslavia, and The Netherlands.

10

In Dallas, Texas, after sundown, cats running in the streets must wear headlights.

11

A cat's gestation period is 55 to 69 days.

12

DON MANUEL OSORIO MANRIQUE DE ZUÑIGA *(detail)*. Francisco José de Goya y Lucientes *(Spanish, 1746–1828); c. 1786–89. Oil on canvas; 50 × 40 in. The Jules Bache Collection, 1949, 49.7.41*

October

13
The cat grimaces, open-mouthed, in response to certain odors. This is known as the Flehmen response.

14
Polydactyl cats have a sixth toe on the inner, thumb side of the foot.

15
When ready to fight, cats straighten their hind legs to look taller, walk slowly and stiffly, bush out their tails, and yowl, growl, and vibrate their lips.

16
The name "tabby" is derived from a section in Baghdad, Iraq, known as Al'attabiya. Here, silk weavers copied the designs and colors of cats coats. Europeans called these textiles "tabby."

17
It is said the Manx lost its tail when Noah unknowingly slammed the door on the cat that was last to board the Ark.

18
Zoologists generally agree that cats have the most delicate sense of touch of all mammals.

19
Highly adaptable, loving, and rugged, the Norwegian Forest Cat is an old breed that appears in Scandinavian legend. Its insulating coat provides natural weatherproofing.

20

Of all domestic animals, cats most willingly abandon themselves to sleep.

21

In magic, the function of the cat has been a lucky charm, a talisman, an amulet, or a mascot.

22

Cats' predatory behavior, especially toward birds, offends many people who find it hard to accept this biological phenomenon.

23

Cats may have four to six kittens in a litter, although Siamese cats may have eight or nine.

24

Felines often detect their owners' arrival before anyone else can. They can hear a person's footsteps or even recognize the sound of certain car engines.

25

The only risk you run in befriending a cat, the writer Colette said, is enriching yourself.

26

Glands that produce scent are located on each side of the cat's forehead and on its lips, chin, and tail. The scent is used to show friendship and mark their territory.

Many Persians like their "thrones" or special places and don't relinquish them easily.

27

The legend of Dick Whittington and his cat is an old favorite in British literature.

28

If a sharp "No!" is ignored by your feline companion, try a squirt from a toy water gun or a spray bottle.

29

Upon discovering three cats suffering with cold in General Grant's camp during the Civil War, Abraham Lincoln adopted them.

30

Cats can't see in the dark, but their pupils shrink to slits in strong light and expand in poor light, allowing a maximum amount of vision in a minimum amount of light.

31

JOSEPH IN PRISON *(detail)*. Master of the Story of Joseph *(Flemish, active , 1500). Tempera and oil on wood; diam. 61½ in. Harris Brisbane Dick Fund, 1953, 53.168*

NOVEMBER

1

The mechanism that enables a cat to purr is not well understood.

2

In Egypt, mummified mice were buried along with the revered mummified cats to provide food in the afterlife.

3

"The cat sees through shut lids."
—*English saying*

4

Cat fanciers learn to accept their pets on their own terms, with love and understanding of their mood swings.

5

At British cat shows, each entrant is thoroughly examined by a veterinarian before it is admitted. "Vetting-in" has generally been discontinued at shows in North America.

"Cat and monkeys, monkeys and cats—all human life is there."
  —*Henry James*

6

Male tortoiseshells, occurring once in every 200 births, are usually sterile.

7

A frightened or disagreeably surprised cat immediately flattens itself as if ready to leap.

8

Leonardo da Vinci once declared that "the small feline is a masterpiece."

9

Normally cats avoid eye contact, but when in the throes of a confrontation with an enemy their gaze is unwavering.

10

Laboratory experiments indicate that felines are ambidextrous.

11

The domestic cat is domestic only as much as it wants to be; it hates to be tied, harnessed, or told when it can come and go.

12

Adjusting the eyes' focus to distance is swift
and precise and enables a cat to gauge jumping
distances exactly.

13

Don't put water or food into your cat's travel
case; it can survive without water for 24 hours
and longer without food.

14

Alexandre Dumas called the cat "an aristocrat
in type and origin whom we have slandered
and ... merits at least our esteem ...."

15

Cat experts estimate that for every cat with a
home there is at least one homeless one
managing on its own.

16

After the popular story *The Life and Adventures
of a Cat*, featuring Tom the cat, was published
in 1760, "tom" came to be the name for the
male of the species.

17

The tailless Manx cat, with origins on the Isle
of Man, is probably the result of a spontaneous
mutation. It has a rabbit-like hop because the
hind legs are longer than the forelegs.

18

Laboratory experiments have shown that cats
can't distinguish the taste of sugar.

19

CAT AND YELLOW BUTTERFLY *(detail)*. Hsü Pei-hung, *or* Ju Péon *(Chinese,
1895–1953). Hanging scroll, ink and color on paper; 44 × 21¼ in.
Rogers Fund, 1956, 56.129.2*

November

20
At full sprint, a domestic cat can run at the rate of 31 miles per hour.

21
Calicos frequently are affectionate and possessive toward their owners but tend to ignore other humans.

22
Pywacket in *Bell, Book and Candle* and Cat in *Breakfast at Tiffany's* are memorable movie stars.

23
Cats easily become part of a household without demanding much of the owner's time.

24
One out of two cats is addicted to catnip, which causes euphoric, uninhibited behavior. Fortunately no permanent negative effects have been reported.

25
Acclimate your cat to car travel at an early age by giving it short, frequent rides.

26
"Watch a cat when it enters the room for the first time. It searches and smells about . . . . It trusts nothing until it has examined . . . everything." —*Rousseau*

27

Objects that give off heat rays attract and hold cats. When the summer sun is gone, they seek the radiator or fireplace.

28

Cats are masters of body language. They express their feelings with their whole bodies, especially their faces and tails.

29

When you visit a cat show, resist the impulse to pet the contestants. Cat exhibitors fear transmission of diseases from contact by people who may have touched other cats.

30

"Cobby" and "oriental" are terms used to describe cats' body types. Cobby means a heavy, rounded, short-legged type, such as the Persians. Orientals are slim and sleek, typified by the Siamese.

DECEMBER

The direct ancestor of the domestic cat,
the African wildcat, was domesticated in
ancient Egypt.

1

The only domesticated form of a true spotted
cat is the rare Egyptian Mau. It bears a close
resemblance to cats observed in ancient
Egyptian artworks.

2

One of the new short-haired breeds is the
spotted Bengal cat. A cross between the
Asian leopard cat and the domestic tabby,
its wild look belies a gentle temperament.

3

Egyptians revered cats for their nobility, their
unorthodoxy, and their almond-shaped eyes.

4

Felines love contact with silk, velvet, and wool
and the softness of real fur.

5

CAT AND SERPENT *(detail). Facsimile of wall painting by unknown
artist (Egyptian, XIX Dynasty); c. 1300 B.C. Copy in tempera by C. K.
Wilkinson, 1920–21; 35 × 19 in. The Metropolitan Museum of Art,
Egyptian Expedition, 30.4.1*

December

6

In England, during World War II, cats would often ask to be put in a safe, protected area just before air raid sirens sounded.

7

Old Possum's Book of Practical Cats, written by T.S. Eliot, was inspired by his fascination with the personalities of cats.

8

Cats are there if you call them—if they don't have anything better to do.

9

Edward Lear's most famous work about cats was his nonsense poem, *The Owl and the Pussycat*.

10

Keep your cat in a well-ventilated travel case and not in a closed car on hot days.

11

Two of Theodore Roosevelt's favorite cats, Tom Quartz and Slippers, frequently appeared at White House state dinners.

12

The Birman, often called the "sacred cat of Burma," is a gentle, easy-going cat that closely resembles the Himalayan except for a shorter coat and a short, white "glove" on each paw.

13

is believed that the Greeks, who learned
f cats' economic value as ratters, stole them
om the Egyptians—who would not sell these
ivine beings—and brought them to Europe.

14

cats suddenly disappeared, it would be only
matter of weeks before rodents completely
verran the world.

15

ats take plenty of exercise, but they never
aste energy.

16

/hy is the cat's curiosity so great that it must
now what's inside every box, paperbag, or
ackage it encounters?

17

n embroidery hanging in Holyrood, England,
epicts a cat (Elizabeth I) playing with a mouse
Mary, Queen of Scots).

18

hen Horace Walpole wrote to his friend
homas Gray that his cat Selima had died, the
oet wrote an ode *On the Death of a Favourite
at, Drowned in a Tub of Gold Fishes.*

19

ome people think dogs superior to cats
ecause cats do not obey easily. A cat won't
imp into a lake and fetch a stick. Would you?

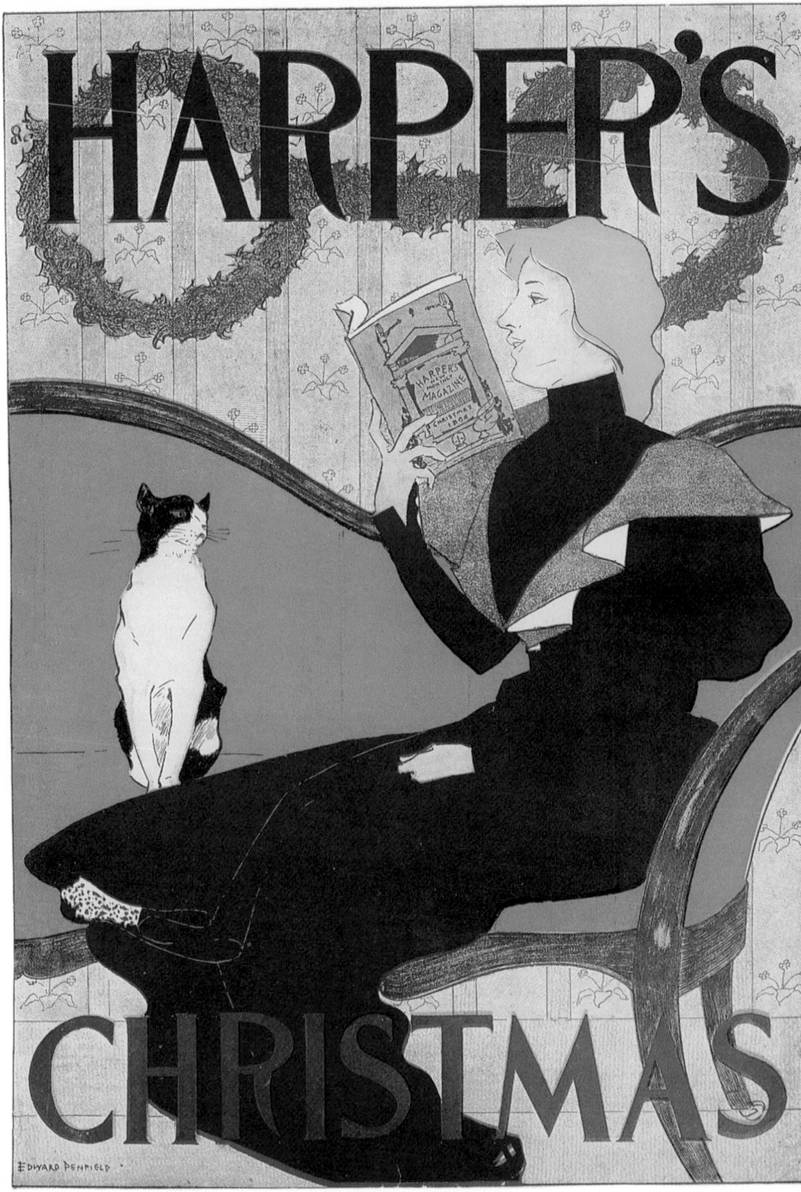
HARPER'S
CHRISTMAS
EDWARD PENFIELD

December

Keeping a cat hungry won't make it a better
hunter. A strong, healthy, alert cat hunts best.

20

"I gave an order to the cat, and the cat gave it
to its tail."
  —*Chinese proverb*

21

Because of the brilliance of their eyes,
Egyptians prized felines as guardians of
precious light and offered them shelter at
nightfall.

22

In the early 18th century, medals were struck
in the cat's honor.

23

The Siamese is said to be the most jealous
of all the cats.

24

Think twice before declawing a cat. A cat
without claws is unable to groom itself,
scamper up a tree, or defend itself when
cornered.

25

Feline beauty was sometimes enhanced by the
Egyptians placing a gold ring in a cat's ear.

26

December

27

"A kitten . . . does not discover that her tail belongs to her until you tread on it."
—*Henry David Thoreau*

28

Cats' eyes glow in the dark because they have a light-reflecting layer at the rear of their eyes.

29

While sleeping, adult cats often purr, chatter their teeth, shiver, or flex their claws, which seem to indicate dreaming.

30

The relationship of the cat and the moon is an idea that probably began in Egypt.

31

Myths surrounding cats' hunting instinct include these: neutered male cats will become fat and lazy and won't hunt; female cats will hunt only when they have a litter of kittens to feed.

	1991	1992	1993	1994
New Year's Day	Jan 1	Jan 1	Jan 1	Jan 1
Martin Luther King, Jr.'s Birthday *(Observed)*	Jan 21	Jan 20	Jan 18	Jan 17
Presidents' Day	Feb 18	Feb 17	Feb 15	Feb 21
Good Friday	Mar 29	Apr 17	Apr 9	Apr 1
Easter	Mar 31	Apr 19	Apr 11	Apr 3
Mother's Day	May 12	May 10	May 9	May 8
Victoria Day *(Canada)*	May 20	May 18	May 24	May 23
Memorial Day *(Observed)*	May 27	May 25	May 31	May 30
Father's Day	Jun 16	Jun 21	Jun 20	Jun 19
Canada Day	Jul 1	Jul 1	Jul 1	Jul 1
Independence Day	Jul 4	Jul 4	Jul 4	Jul 4
Labor Day	Sep 2	Sep 7	Sep 6	Sep 5
Columbus Day	Oct 14	Oct 12	Oct 11	Oct 10
Thanksgiving Day *(Canada)*	Oct 14	Oct 12	Oct 11	Oct 10
Veterans' Day	Nov 11	Nov 11	Nov 11	Nov 11
Thanksgiving Day	Nov 28	Nov 26	Nov 25	Nov 24
Christmas Day	Dec 25	Dec 25	Dec 25	Dec 25
Boxing Day *(Canada)*	Dec 26	Dec 26	Dec 26	Dec 26

	1995	1996	1997	1998
New Year's Day	Jan 1	Jan 1	Jan 1	Jan 1
Martin Luther King, Jr.'s Birthday *(Observed)*	Jan 16	Jan 15	Jan 20	Jan 18
Presidents' Day	Feb 20	Feb 19	Feb 17	Feb 16
Good Friday	Apr 14	Apr 5	Mar 28	Apr 10
Easter	Apr 16	Apr 7	Mar 30	Apr 12
Mother's Day	May 14	May 12	May 11	May 10
Victoria Day *(Canada)*	May 22	May 20	May 19	May 18
Memorial Day *(Observed)*	May 29	May 27	May 26	May 25
Father's Day	Jun 18	Jun 16	Jun 15	Jun 21
Canada Day	Jul 1	Jul 1	Jul 1	Jul 1
Independence Day	Jul 4	Jul 4	Jul 4	Jul 4
Labor Day	Sep 4	Sep 2	Sep 1	Sep 7
Columbus Day	Oct 9	Oct 14	Oct 13	Oct 12
Thanksgiving Day *(Canada)*	Oct 9	Oct 14	Oct 13	Oct 12
Veterans' Day	Nov 11	Nov 11	Nov 11	Nov 11
Thanksgiving Day	Nov 23	Nov 28	Nov 27	Nov 26
Christmas Day	Dec 25	Dec 25	Dec 25	Dec 25
Boxing Day *(Canada)*	Dec 26	Dec 26	Dec 26	Dec 26

1991

	S	M	T	W	T	F	S
JAN			1	2	3	4	5
	6	7	8	9	10	11	12
	13	14	15	16	17	18	19
	20	**21**	22	23	24	25	26
	27	28	29	30	31		

	S	M	T	W	T	F	S
FEB						1	2
	3	4	5	6	7	8	9
	10	11	12	13	14	15	16
	17	**18**	19	20	21	22	23
	24	25	26	27	28		

	S	M	T	W	T	F	S
MAR						1	2
	3	4	5	6	7	8	9
	10	11	12	13	14	15	16
	17	18	19	20	21	22	23
	24/**31**	25	26	27	28	**29**	30

	S	M	T	W	T	F	S
APR		1	2	3	4	5	6
	7	8	9	10	11	12	13
	14	15	16	17	18	19	20
	21	22	23	24	25	26	27
	28	29	30				

	S	M	T	W	T	F	S
MAY				1	2	3	4
	5	6	7	8	9	10	11
	12	13	14	15	16	17	18
	19	**20**	21	22	23	24	25
	26	**27**	28	29	30	31	

	S	M	T	W	T	F	S
JUN							1
	2	3	4	5	6	7	8
	9	10	11	12	13	14	15
	16	17	18	19	20	21	22
	23/30	24	25	26	27	28	29

	S	M	T	W	T	F	S
JUL		**1**	2	3	**4**	5	6
	7	8	9	10	11	12	13
	14	15	16	17	18	19	20
	21	22	23	24	25	26	27
	28	29	30	31			

	S	M	T	W	T	F	S
AUG					1	2	3
	4	5	6	7	8	9	10
	11	12	13	14	15	16	17
	18	19	20	21	22	23	24
	25	26	27	28	29	30	31

	S	M	T	W	T	F	S
SEP	1	**2**	3	4	5	6	7
	8	9	10	11	12	13	14
	15	16	17	18	19	20	21
	22	23	24	25	26	27	28
	29	30					

	S	M	T	W	T	F	S
OCT			1	2	3	4	5
	6	7	8	9	10	11	12
	13	**14**	15	16	17	18	19
	20	21	22	23	24	25	26
	27	28	29	30	31		

	S	M	T	W	T	F	S
NOV						1	2
	3	4	5	6	7	8	9
	10	**11**	12	13	14	15	16
	17	18	19	20	21	22	23
	24	25	26	27	**28**	29	30

	S	M	T	W	T	F	S
DEC	1	2	3	4	5	6	7
	8	9	10	11	12	13	14
	15	16	17	18	19	20	21
	22	23	24	**25**	**26**	27	28
	29	30	31				

1992

	S	M	T	W	T	F	S
JAN				**1**	2	3	4
	5	6	7	8	9	10	11
	12	13	14	15	16	17	18
	19	**20**	21	22	23	24	25
	26	27	28	29	30	31	
FEB							1
	2	3	4	5	6	7	8
	9	10	11	12	13	14	15
	16	**17**	18	19	20	21	22
	23	24	25	26	27	28	29
MAR	1	2	3	4	5	6	7
	8	9	10	11	12	13	14
	15	16	17	18	19	20	21
	22	23	24	25	26	27	28
	29	30	31				
APR				1	2	3	4
	5	6	7	8	9	10	11
	12	13	14	15	16	**17**	18
	19	20	21	22	23	24	25
	26	27	28	29	30		
MAY						1	2
	3	4	5	6	7	8	9
	10	11	12	13	14	15	16
	17	**18**	19	20	21	22	23
	$^{24}/_{31}$	**25**	26	27	28	29	30
JUN		1	2	3	4	5	6
	7	8	9	10	11	12	13
	14	15	16	17	18	19	20
	21	22	23	24	25	26	27
	28	29	30				

	S	M	T	W	T	F	S
JUL				**1**	2	3	**4**
	5	6	7	8	9	10	11
	12	13	14	15	16	17	18
	19	20	21	22	23	24	25
	26	27	28	29	30	31	
AUG							1
	2	3	4	5	6	7	8
	9	10	11	12	13	14	15
	16	17	18	19	20	21	22
	$^{23}/_{30}$	$^{24}/_{31}$	25	26	27	28	29
SEP			1	2	3	4	5
	6	**7**	8	9	10	11	12
	13	14	15	16	17	18	19
	20	21	22	23	24	25	26
	27	28	29	30			
OCT					1	2	3
	4	5	6	7	8	9	10
	11	**12**	13	14	15	16	17
	18	19	20	21	22	23	24
	25	26	27	28	29	30	31
NOV	1	2	3	4	5	6	7
	8	9	10	**11**	12	13	14
	15	16	17	18	19	20	21
	22	23	24	25	**26**	27	28
	29	30					
DEC			1	2	3	4	5
	6	7	8	9	10	11	12
	13	14	15	16	17	18	19
	20	21	22	23	24	**25**	**26**
	27	28	29	30	31		

1993

	S	M	T	W	T	F	S
JAN						**1**	2
	3	4	5	6	7	8	9
	10	11	12	13	14	15	16
	17	**18**	19	20	21	22	23
	24/31	25	26	27	28	29	30
FEB		1	2	3	4	5	6
	7	8	9	10	11	12	13
	14	**15**	16	17	18	19	20
	21	22	23	24	25	26	27
	28						
MAR		1	2	3	4	5	6
	7	8	9	10	11	12	13
	14	15	16	17	18	19	20
	21	22	23	24	25	26	27
	28	29	30	31			
APR					1	2	3
	4	5	6	7	8	**9**	10
	11	12	13	14	15	16	17
	18	19	20	21	22	23	24
	25	26	27	28	29	30	
MAY							1
	2	3	4	5	6	7	8
	9	10	11	12	13	14	15
	16	17	18	19	20	21	22
	23/30	24/31	25	26	27	28	29
JUN			1	2	3	4	5
	6	7	8	9	10	11	12
	13	14	15	16	17	18	19
	20	21	22	23	24	25	26
	27	28	29	30			

	S	M	T	W	T	F	S
JUL					**1**	2	3
	4	5	6	7	8	9	10
	11	12	13	14	15	16	17
	18	19	20	21	22	23	24
	25	26	27	28	29	30	31
AUG	1	2	3	4	5	6	7
	8	9	10	11	12	13	14
	15	16	17	18	19	20	21
	22	23	24	25	26	27	28
	29	30	31				
SEP			1	2	3	4	
	5	**6**	7	8	9	10	11
	12	13	14	15	16	17	18
	19	20	21	22	23	24	25
	26	27	28	29	30		
OCT						1	2
	3	4	5	6	7	8	9
	10	**11**	12	13	14	15	16
	17	18	19	20	21	22	23
	24/31	25	26	27	28	29	30
NOV		1	2	3	4	5	6
	7	8	9	10	**11**	12	13
	14	15	16	17	18	19	20
	21	22	23	24	**25**	26	27
	28	29	30				
DEC			1	2	3	4	
	5	6	7	8	9	10	11
	12	13	14	15	16	17	18
	19	20	21	22	23	24	**25**
	26	27	28	29	30	31	

EGYPTIAN CAT, *Unknown artist (Egyptian, Late Dynastic period, 950–350 B.C.). Statue, hollow-cast bronze; 4¾ × 3 in. Fletcher Fund, 1966 and The Guide Foundation Inc. Gift, 1966, 66.99.145*

1994

	S	M	T	W	T	F	S
JAN							**1**
	2	3	4	5	6	7	8
	9	10	11	12	13	14	15
	16	**17**	18	19	20	21	22
	23/30	24/31	25	26	27	28	29

FEB			1	2	3	4	5
	6	7	8	9	10	11	12
	13	14	15	16	17	18	19
	20	**21**	22	23	24	25	26
	27	28					

MAR			1	2	3	4	5
	6	7	8	9	10	11	12
	13	14	15	16	17	18	19
	20	21	22	23	24	25	26
	27	28	29	30	31		

APR						**1**	2
	3	4	5	6	7	8	9
	10	11	12	13	14	15	16
	17	18	19	20	21	22	23
	24	25	26	27	28	29	30

MAY	1	2	3	4	5	6	7
	8	9	10	11	12	13	14
	15	16	17	18	19	20	21
	22	**23**	24	25	26	27	28
	29	**30**	31				

JUN				1	2	3	4
	5	6	7	8	9	10	11
	12	13	14	15	16	17	18
	19	20	21	22	23	24	25
	26	27	28	29	30		

	S	M	T	W	T	F	S
JUL						**1**	2
	3	**4**	5	6	7	8	9
	10	11	12	13	14	15	16
	17	18	19	20	21	22	23
	24/31	25	26	27	28	29	30

AUG		1	2	3	4	5	6
	7	8	9	10	11	12	13
	14	15	16	17	18	19	20
	21	22	23	24	25	26	27
	28	29	30	31			

SEP					1	2	3
	4	**5**	6	7	8	9	10
	11	12	13	14	15	16	17
	18	19	20	21	22	23	24
	25	26	27	28	29	30	

OCT							1
	2	3	4	5	6	7	8
	9	**10**	11	12	13	14	15
	16	17	18	19	20	21	22
	23/30	24/31	25	26	27	28	29

NOV			1	2	3	4	5
	6	7	8	9	10	**11**	12
	13	14	15	16	17	18	19
	20	21	22	23	**24**	25	26
	27	28	29	30			

DEC			1	2	3		
	4	5	6	7	8	9	10
	11	12	13	14	15	16	17
	18	19	20	21	22	23	24
	25	**26**	27	28	29	30	31

1995

	S	M	T	W	T	F	S
JAN	**1**	2	3	4	5	6	7
	8	9	10	11	12	13	14
	15	**16**	17	18	19	20	21
	22	23	24	25	26	27	28
	29	30	31				

	S	M	T	W	T	F	S
FEB				1	2	3	4
	5	6	7	8	9	10	11
	12	13	14	15	16	17	18
	19	**20**	21	22	23	24	25
	26	27	28				

	S	M	T	W	T	F	S
MAR				1	2	3	4
	5	6	7	8	9	10	11
	12	13	14	15	16	17	18
	19	20	21	22	23	24	25
	26	27	28	29	30	31	

	S	M	T	W	T	F	S
APR							1
	2	3	4	5	6	7	8
	9	10	11	12	13	**14**	15
	16	17	18	19	20	21	22
	23/30	24	25	26	27	28	29

	S	M	T	W	T	F	S
MAY		1	2	3	4	5	6
	7	8	9	10	11	12	13
	14	15	16	17	18	19	20
	21	**22**	23	24	25	26	27
	28	**29**	30	31			

	S	M	T	W	T	F	S
JUN					1	2	3
	4	5	6	7	8	9	10
	11	12	13	14	15	16	17
	18	19	20	21	22	23	24
	25	26	27	28	29	30	

	S	M	T	W	T	F	S
JUL							**1**
	2	3	**4**	5	6	7	8
	9	10	11	12	13	14	15
	16	17	18	19	20	21	22
	23/30	24/31	25	26	27	28	29

	S	M	T	W	T	F	S
AUG			1	2	3	4	5
	6	7	8	9	10	11	12
	13	14	15	16	17	18	19
	20	21	22	23	24	25	26
	27	28	29	30	31		

	S	M	T	W	T	F	S
SEP						1	2
	3	**4**	5	6	7	8	9
	10	11	12	13	14	15	16
	17	18	19	20	21	22	23
	24	25	26	27	28	29	30

	S	M	T	W	T	F	S
OCT	1	2	3	4	5	6	7
	8	**9**	10	11	12	13	14
	15	16	17	18	19	20	21
	22	23	24	25	26	27	28
	29	30	31				

	S	M	T	W	T	F	S
NOV				1	2	3	4
	5	6	7	8	9	10	**11**
	12	13	14	15	16	17	18
	19	20	21	22	**23**	24	25
	26	27	28	29	30		

	S	M	T	W	T	F	S
DEC						1	2
	3	4	5	6	7	8	9
	10	11	12	13	14	15	16
	17	18	19	20	21	22	23
	24/31	**25**	**26**	27	28	29	30

1996

	S	M	T	W	T	F	S
JAN		**1**	2	3	4	5	6
	7	8	9	10	11	12	13
	14	**15**	16	17	18	19	20
	21	22	23	24	25	26	27
	28	29	30	31			
FEB					1	2	3
	4	5	6	7	8	9	10
	11	12	13	14	15	16	17
	18	**19**	20	21	22	23	24
	25	26	27	28	29		
MAR						1	2
	3	4	5	6	7	8	9
	10	11	12	13	14	15	16
	17	18	19	20	21	22	23
	24/31	25	26	27	28	29	30
APR		1	2	3	4	**5**	6
	7	8	9	10	11	12	13
	14	15	16	17	18	19	20
	21	22	23	24	25	26	27
	28	29	30				
MAY				1	2	3	4
	5	6	7	8	9	10	11
	12	13	14	15	16	17	18
	19	**20**	21	22	23	24	25
	26	**27**	28	29	30	31	
JUN							1
	2	3	4	5	6	7	8
	9	10	11	12	13	14	15
	16	17	18	19	20	21	22
	23/30	24	25	26	27	28	29

	S	M	T	W	T	F	S
JUL		**1**	2	3	**4**	5	6
	7	8	9	10	11	12	13
	14	15	16	17	18	19	20
	21	22	23	24	25	26	27
	28	29	30	31			
AUG					1	2	3
	4	5	6	7	8	9	10
	11	12	13	14	15	16	17
	18	19	20	21	22	23	24
	25	26	27	28	29	30	31
SEP	1	**2**	3	4	5	6	7
	8	9	10	11	12	13	14
	15	16	17	18	19	20	21
	22	23	24	25	26	27	28
	29	30					
OCT			1	2	3	4	5
	6	7	8	9	10	11	12
	13	**14**	15	16	17	18	19
	20	21	22	23	24	25	26
	27	28	29	30	31		
NOV						1	2
	3	4	5	6	7	8	9
	10	**11**	12	13	14	15	16
	17	18	19	20	21	22	23
	24	25	26	27	**28**	29	30
DEC	1	2	3	4	5	6	7
	8	9	10	11	12	13	14
	15	16	17	18	19	20	21
	22	23	24	**25**	**26**	27	28
	29	30	31				

EMMA HOMAN *(detail)*. John Bradley *(American, active 1832–1847); 1843/44. Oil on canvas; 33⅞ × 27⅛ in. Gift of Edgar William and Bernice Chrysler Garbisch, 1966, 66.242.23*

1997

	S	M	T	W	T	F	S
JAN				**1**	2	3	4
	5	6	7	8	9	10	11
	12	13	14	15	16	17	18
	19	**20**	21	22	23	24	25
	26	27	28	29	30	31	

	S	M	T	W	T	F	S
FEB							1
	2	3	4	5	6	7	8
	9	10	11	12	13	14	15
	16	**17**	18	19	20	21	22
	23	24	25	26	27	28	

	S	M	T	W	T	F	S
MAR							1
	2	3	4	5	6	7	8
	9	10	11	12	13	14	15
	16	17	18	19	20	21	22
	23/30	24/31	25	26	27	**28**	29

	S	M	T	W	T	F	S
APR			1	2	3	4	5
	6	7	8	9	10	11	12
	13	14	15	16	17	18	19
	20	21	22	23	24	25	26
	27	28	29	30			

	S	M	T	W	T	F	S
MAY					1	2	3
	4	5	6	7	8	9	10
	11	12	13	14	15	16	17
	18	**19**	20	21	22	23	24
	25	**26**	27	28	29	30	31

	S	M	T	W	T	F	S
JUN	1	2	3	4	5	6	7
	8	9	10	11	12	13	14
	15	16	17	18	19	20	21
	22	23	24	25	26	27	28
	29	30					

	S	M	T	W	T	F	S
JUL			**1**	2	3	**4**	5
	6	7	8	9	10	11	12
	13	14	15	16	17	18	19
	20	21	22	23	24	25	26
	27	28	29	30	31		

	S	M	T	W	T	F	S
AUG						1	2
	3	4	5	6	7	8	9
	10	11	12	13	14	15	16
	17	18	19	20	21	22	23
	24/31	25	26	27	28	29	30

	S	M	T	W	T	F	S
SEP		**1**	2	3	4	5	6
	7	8	9	10	11	12	13
	14	15	16	17	18	19	20
	21	22	23	24	25	26	27
	28	29	30				

	S	M	T	W	T	F	S
OCT				1	2	3	4
	5	6	7	8	9	10	11
	12	**13**	14	15	16	17	18
	19	20	21	22	23	24	25
	26	27	28	29	30	31	

	S	M	T	W	T	F	S
NOV							1
	2	3	4	5	6	7	8
	9	10	**11**	12	13	14	15
	16	17	18	19	20	21	22
	23/30	24	25	26	**27**	28	29

	S	M	T	W	T	F	S
DEC		1	2	3	4	5	6
	7	8	9	10	11	12	13
	14	15	16	17	18	19	20
	21	22	23	24	**25**	**26**	27
	28	29	30	31			

1998

	S	M	T	W	T	F	S
JAN					**1**	2	3
	4	5	6	7	8	9	10
	11	12	13	14	15	16	17
	18	19	20	21	22	23	24
	25	26	27	28	29	30	31
FEB	1	2	3	4	5	6	7
	8	9	10	11	12	13	14
	15	**16**	17	18	19	20	21
	22	23	24	25	26	27	28
MAR	1	2	3	4	5	6	7
	8	9	10	11	12	13	14
	15	16	17	18	19	20	21
	22	23	24	25	26	27	28
	29	30	31				
APR			1	2	3	4	
	5	6	7	8	9	**10**	11
	12	13	14	15	16	17	18
	19	20	21	22	23	24	25
	26	27	28	29	30		
MAY						1	2
	3	4	5	6	7	8	9
	10	11	12	13	14	15	16
	17	**18**	19	20	21	22	23
	$^{24}/_{31}$	**25**	26	27	28	29	30
JUN		1	2	3	4	5	6
	7	8	9	10	11	12	13
	14	15	16	17	18	19	20
	21	22	23	24	25	26	27
	28	29	30				

	S	M	T	W	T	F	S
JUL				**1**	2	3	**4**
	5	6	7	8	9	10	11
	12	13	14	15	16	17	18
	19	20	21	22	23	24	25
	26	27	28	29	30	31	
AUG							1
	2	3	4	5	6	7	8
	9	10	11	12	13	14	15
	16	17	18	19	20	21	22
	$^{23}/_{30}$	$^{24}/_{31}$	25	26	27	28	29
SEP			1	2	3	4	5
	6	**7**	8	9	10	11	12
	13	14	15	16	17	18	19
	20	21	22	23	24	25	26
	27	28	29	30			
OCT					1	2	3
	4	5	6	7	8	9	10
	11	**12**	13	14	15	16	17
	18	19	20	21	22	23	24
	25	26	27	28	29	30	31
NOV	1	2	3	4	5	6	7
	8	9	10	**11**	12	13	14
	15	16	17	18	19	20	21
	22	23	24	25	**26**	27	28
	29	30					
DEC			1	2	3	4	5
	6	7	8	9	10	11	12
	13	14	15	16	17	18	19
	20	21	22	23	24	**25**	**26**
	27	28	29	30	31		

Name	Address	Telephone Number
		A
		B

Name	Address	Telephone Number

C
D

Name	Address	Telephone Number

E
F

Name	Address	Telephone Number

G
H

CERAMIC CAT, *Anonymous modeler (English, 17th century). Tin-enameled earthenware; 4¼ × 5⅜ in. Gift of Mrs. Russell S. Carter, 1945, 45.12.5*

Name	*Address*	*Telephone Number*

I
J

Name	Address	Telephone Number

K
L

Name	Address	Telephone Number

PETIT CHAT *(detail)*. Tsugouhara Foujita *(French, 1886–1968); 1926. Pen and black ink, gray wash; 6¼ × 8⅝ in. Bequest of Miss Adelaide Milton de Groot (1876–1967), 1967, 67.187.7*

Name	Address	Telephone Number

O
P
Q

Name	Address	Telephone Number

R
S

Name	Address	Telephone Number

T
U

Name	Address	Telephone Number

V
W

Name	Address	Telephone Number

X
Y
Z

SEATED CAT *(detail).* Chu Ling *(Chinese, 19th century); c. 1800.*
Hanging scroll, ink and color on paper; 36⅞ × 14½ in. Rogers
Fund, 1956, 56.129.3

COMPAGNIE FRANÇAISE DES CHOCOLATS ET DES THÈS *(detail).* Théophile-Alexandre Steinlen *(French, 1859–1923); 1899. Color lithograph poster; 30 × 40 in. Gift of Bessie Potter Vonnoh, 1941, 41.12.19*

SPRING PLAY IN A T'ANG GARDEN *(detail). Style of Hsüan-tsung (Chinese, 1398–1435); 18th century. Handscroll, colors on silk; 14¾ × 104 in. Fletcher Fund, 1947, 47.18.9*